Pumpkin & Squash

Elaine Elliot & Virginia Lee

Formac Publishing Company Limited
Halifax

In continuing the theme of the Flavours series of cookbooks, we have invited chefs from across Canada to share their recipes, and we thank them for their generosity. Each recipe has been tested and adjusted for the home cook.
— *Elaine Elliot and Virginia Lee*

Special thanks to **Craig Flinn**, chef and proprietor of Chives Canadian Bistro in Halifax, for preparing and styling many of the recipes photographed for this book.

Thanks also to the staff at Art Can Gallery, Deco Restaurant, Kellock's Restaurant, Restaurant Le Caveau, Saege Bistro/Scanway Catering, Tempest Restaurant, and the Westin Nova Scotian Hotel for their help in preparing dishes for photography on location.

Participating restaurants

British Columbia
Bishop's Restaurant, Vancouver, BC
Raincity Grill, Vancouver, BC
Sequoia Grill at the Teahouse, Vancouver, BC

New Brunswick
The Blue Door Restaurant, Fredericton, NB
San Martello Dining Room at the Dufferin Inn, Saint John, NB
Sunset on the River Bed & Breakfast, Upper Kingsclear, NB

Nova Scotia
Arbor View Inn, Lunenburg, NS
Art Can Gallery, Canning, NS
Blomidon Inn, Wolfville, NS
Deco Restaurant, Halifax, NS
Le Caveau at Domaine de Grand Pré, Grand Pré, NS
Evangeline Inn and Café, Grand Pré, NS
Fireside Café, Canning, NS
Inn on the Lake, Waverley, NS

Kellock's Restaurant, Berwick, NS
Keltic Lodge, Ingonish Beach, NS
Lobster Shack Restaurant at Salmon River House
Country Inn, Salmon River Bridge, NS
The Old Orchard Inn, Greenwich, NS
Paddy's Pub, Kentville, NS
Scanway Catering, Halifax, NS
Tempest Restaurant, Wolfville, NS
Westin Nova Scotian Hotel, Halifax, NS

Ontario
Hillebrand's Vineyard Café, Niagara-on-the-Lake, ON
Jakobstettel Inn, St. Jacobs, ON
Peller Estates Winery, Niagara-on-the-Lake, ON
Vineland Estates, Vineland, ON
Westover Inn, St. Marys, ON

Quebec
Restaurant Les Fougères, Chelsea, QC

For Library and Archives Canada Cataloguing in Publication information, please see p.96

Copyright © 2006 Formac Publishing Company
All rights reserved. No part of this book may be reproduced or transmitted in any form or by any means, electronic or mechanical, including photocopying, or by any information storage or retrieval system, without permission in writing from the publisher.

Formac Publishing Company Limited recognizes the support of the Province of Nova Scotia through the Department of Tourism, Culture and Heritage. We acknowledge the financial support of the Government of Canada through the Book Publishing Industry Development Program (BPIDP) for our publishing activities.

Formac Publishing Company Limited
5502 Atlantic Street
Halifax, Nova Scotia B3H 1G4
www.formac.ca

Printed and bound in Canada

Contents

Introduction

Pumpkins, those golden globes of the squash family, are woven into the folklore and traditions of our lives. From childhood nursery rhymes to the Hallowe'en jack-o'-lantern and the obligatory Thanksgiving pumpkin pie piled high with thick whipped cream, we are tied to this native New World fruit. What would autumn be without the pumpkin?

Pumpkin. Squash. What's the difference? Well, not much — they are all in the same family. Pumpkins and squash belong to the cucurbitaceae or gourd family which also includes cucumbers, zucchini, watermelon, cantaloupe and honeydew melons. Cucurbits are native to most of the world's countries and, with the exception of Antarctica, grow on all continents, especially those with tropical climates. But we can claim the pumpkin as our own.

The species squash is native to the Western Hemisphere and records show their consumption as far back as 5000 BCE; squash seeds have been excavated from Mexican habitation sites dating back 7000 years. Squash were planted by Native North Americans and, like maize, were a major food crop in the area. Graciously given by Native Americans to European explorers, these plants in turn became a dietary staple of settlers in the New World.

In fact, these settlers gave the pumpkin its name. It is thought that the French explorer Jacques Cartier, while exploring the St. Lawrence region in 1584, happened upon the squash, a fruit 'new to his experience.' To his eye it looked like a huge melon — called *pompon* in French. Pompon was derived from the Greek *pepon* meaning large melon. In Elizabethan English it was called *pumpion*; Shakespeare referred to it in *The Merry Wives of Windsor.* The word eventually evolved into pumpkin, the name we use today for the round, orange variety of the squash species with the strong Hallowe'en association.

There are several cultivated squash species and maybe a thousand named varieties. As there is very little botanical difference between squashes of different species, they are often referred to simply as summer squash and winter squash. Pumpkin and squash may be used interchangeably in many recipes, especially baked goods like quick breads, cakes or cookies.

It is easy to identify cultivated members of the cucurbita family; however, it is not easy to distinguish among plants within the family — squash and cucumber and melon plants look pretty much the same. They all grow on vines with five-lobed leaves arranged alternately on the stem and spread by spring-like tendrils. The large, flat seeds are attached to the inside wall (ovary) of the fruit. The seeds, called pepitas, are edible and some squash are grown specifically for the seeds. The five-petal flowers are also edible and in some Mediterranean cultures considered a delicacy. In Medici-era Florence the flowers were served at special feasts. Pumpkin and other squash fruit typically have a tough skin and yellow or orange flesh rich in carotenoids. Unlike soft-skinned summer squash that are eaten when immature, winter squash, including pumpkin, are harvested when fully ripe. Winter squash are drier and sweeter, and have a tough indigestible skin. Winter squash may be stored in a cool, dry place for up to six months, making them an important part of the winter diet. In the old days they were often kept under the beds!

Pumpkin and other winter squash are monoecious — they produce both male (staminate) and female (pistillate) flowers on the same plant. The first flowers of the season are usually non-fruiting male staminate flowers, followed by female pistillate flowers several weeks later. The male flowers provide pollen for female flower germination. Female flowers are only receptive to pollination for approximately 24 hours. Beehives are often placed in pumpkin fields during the bloom period to ensure adequate pollination for the production of an economical crop.

Most pumpkins require a growing period of 120 days to maturity. Pumpkins are grown almost everywhere in Canada, although only a few are grown on the prairies where generally the growing season is not long enough. Pumpkins and other squash are fairly easy to grow. They don't have particular soil requirements though fertile, well-drained soil is usually a given. They like some wind protection, and they do need a lot of space (approximately one to two square metres per plant, depending on variety). Seeds are sown or, in home gardens, nursery seedlings are often transplanted, when all danger of frost is passed. Squash plants

decorations, jack-o'-lanterns, giant pumpkin competitions, pies and other baked goods, and preserves. The remaining 10% are processed into pure canned pumpkin, canned pumpkin pie filling, baby foods, seeds for reproduction — nursery and packaged seed markets, and seeds for snack foods. Pumpkins for processing are grown in Ontario, Quebec and New Brunswick. One of the major producers is E.D.Smith and Sons Limited of Winona, ON; their pumpkin pie filling is legendary, and their pure pumpkin is popular with those requiring a gluten-free diet.

In recent years pumpkins have become Canada's fastest-growing vegetable crop. Since 1986 the acreage devoted to pumpkin cultivation has doubled and pumpkins have risen in the ranks from fifteenth to seventh most important vegetable crop. In 2001 there were two square metres of pumpkin planted for every person in Canada, producing a crop worth $22 million to producers. While that is a far cry from the number one–ranked potato at $961 million, the humble gourd has become an agricultural phenomenon to be reckoned with.

Why has the pumpkin taken such a leap in the popularity polls? There are several reasons and basically they boil down to marketing, marketing and marketing. The first would be the great commercialization of Thanksgiving and Hallowe'en. Hallowe'en is second only to Christmas as the holiday on which Canadians spend the most money for cards, gifts, costumes and decorations. The pumpkin, the very symbol of Hallowe'en, has been the beneficiary of big

tolerate a fair amount of drought but may require some irrigation during extended dry periods in early summer. They may rot if too wet towards the end of the growing season. Squash must be harvested when fully ripe but before repeated frosts or exposure to too much rain. Pumpkins and fresh-market squash are picked by hand. Machinery is used to assist in the harvesting of fruit for storage and processing. Pumpkins and winter squash that are being stored for later fresh sale or destined for processing are dried off and quickly cooled, then boxed and trucked to their respective destinations.

About 90% of all pumpkins grown are marketed fresh for ornamental use in seasonal

retail marketing.

Next is the emergence of agri-tourism as an important adjunct to some agricultural operations. City dwellers in ever-increasing numbers are flocking to the countryside to partake of the farm experience. Pumpkin farmers, particularly those with farms within easy access of major urban centres (such as Toronto, Montreal and Vancouver) are expanding their operations to include agri-tourism activities, which are often promoted by tourism departments. Pick-your-own pumpkin patches offer wheelbarrows, giant pumpkin displays, pumpkin carving, haunted barns, hay rides and more. Fresh pumpkins and pumpkin pies as well as other home-baked goods, fresh

produce and local crafts are often sold in adjacent farm markets. Pumpkins have come a long way from the roadside stand of yore, and pumpkin farmers benefit from this alternative source of income.

Finally, but no less significant, is the rise of the great pumpkin, which can be attributed to one man. Howard Dill of Windsor, N.S., broke the Guinness world record for largest pumpkin in 1979 and for several years thereafter. Dill's "Atlantic Giant" *pvp* pumpkin seeds, patented in 1986, have been breaking world records ever since. Giant pumpkins have become an industry in their own right. The enthusiasm (and the seed) has spread worldwide. Howard Dill's seeds have produced pumpkins of record weights

from Pennsylvania to Germany. Competitions and festivals draw great crowds and plenty of media coverage. Clubs and weigh-offs have gone international. Organizers meet annually in Niagara Falls to swap seeds and stories, and to plan new events and strategies.

Every little princess in Canada knows that big pumpkins can become beautiful horse-drawn coaches — so why not boats as well? Yes, pumpkin regattas are becoming the rage, and while skippers have not as yet included royalty, celebrities and local officials are taking to the seas in hollowed giant gourds-cum-gondolas. The first such Pumpkin Regatta was raced, fittingly, in Windsor. The pumpkin has captured the popular imagination, and gourd growers rejoice.

Pumpkins range in size from miniature to mammoth. Tiny pumpkins appeal to little people. They are also popular for table decorations and arrangements. Medium-sized pumpkins are sold mostly for Hallowe'en jack-o'-lanterns, and some go to processing. Giant pumpkins are featured attractions at county fairs across the land and have contributed mightily to the growth of the gourd's popularity. At the Vancouver Island Pumpkin Festival, the world's largest pumpkin pie made 1000 servings.

Pumpkins are so attractive that one always buys more than one actually needs. So what do you do with all those pumpkins you bought at the pumpkin patch? Pumpkin carving has evolved into an art form, not just a scary face.

At the annual Scarecrow Festival in Mahone Bay, N.S., hundreds of beautifully carved themed pumpkins form a Pumpkin Path that draws thousands of evening strollers. You too can carve your own Picassos from pumpkins. Kids can participate in the fun by drawing on the faces or designs with magic marker. An adult then does the carving. Children can help scrape out the seeds, arrange them on a baking sheet and sprinkle them with salt. After the seeds are baked crisp, a tasty and wholesome snack is enjoyed. Youngsters may even dry some seeds and save them to plant their own. Pumpkins are an exciting starter crop for young gardeners. Even if the crop consists of only one pumpkin, the reward is great.

And you can always make lots of pies or cookies or sweet breads. Cook, purée and freeze the pumpkin for future baking.

When selecting squash, choose fruit that have a good three inches (eight cm) of stem intact (if the stem is broken off the fruit will spoil quickly), are heavy for their size and have dull-coloured skin. Avoid those with soft spots and cracks. Squash are available year-round, with the peak season from early fall until early winter. They can be stored for several months in a cool, dry, dark location, ideally around 55°F (12°C). Cut squash can be stored wrapped in plastic and refrigerated up to five days. Cooked squash should be stored in airtight containers in the refrigerator for no longer than five days, or frozen for longer storage.

Since squash lie on the ground it is important to wash them under cold running water until all grit is removed. The cooking method you choose will depend upon the way you plan to serve the squash. Small squash like Acorn will be baked unpeeled, cut in half or wedges. Cubed squash will be pared before cooking. Squash or pumpkin that you plan to purée may be cooked with the skin off, or with the skin on and the flesh removed and puréed when cool. If you plan to bake a whole unpeeled squash, remember to pierce the skin in several places to allow steam to escape.

Cutting squash can be a challenge, as the rind of many varieties is extremely tough. Use a cleaver or a large knife to cut the squash or pumpkin in half; it may be necessary to hammer

the cleaver with a mallet. Alternatively, punch a couple of holes in the squash and microwave until the rind is soft enough to cut. Using a large spoon, remove the seeds and stringy fibers from the cavity.

The bright orange colour of pumpkin flesh is a clear indication of its superior nutritional value — the deeper the colour, the greater the presence of beta-carotene. One cup of baked, unsalted pumpkin or squash contains between 49 and 82 calories, two grams of protein and no fat. It is an excellent source of vitamin A, and a good source of vitamin C, magnesium, potassium and dietary fibre. The vitamin A (beta-carotene) found abundantly in pumpkin and winter squash is purported to reduce the risk of developing certain types of cancer. Beta-carotene is also thought to offer protection against heart disease and some degenerative aspects of aging. Pumpkin also provides smaller amounts of nutrients important to a well-rounded diet: calcium, iron, zinc, niacin, folate and vitamin E.

The pumpkin's round shape resembling a human head makes it a prime object in the tomfoolery of folklore. How appropriate that Cinderella should arrive at the ball in a gigantic, perfectly formed, golden carriage conjured from a lowly pumpkin out of the family garden. Where else would Peter the Pumpkin Eater imprison his wayward wife but in a large hollowed-out pumpkin? And would Washington Irving's tale of Ichabod Crane in *The Legend of Sleepy Hollow* be quite so scary without the hurled pumpkin? The mere thought that a jack-o'-lantern could be used to imitate a human head is absolutely frightening, especially on Hallowe'en.

Nowhere is the folklore of the pumpkin more apparent than in the spooky jack-o'-lanterns of Hallowe'en night — candle-lit pumpkins with scary faces carved into them displayed to chase away ghosts that according to legend return each All Hallows Eve. Irish immigrants brought this tradition to the Americas. In Celtic folklore, a character named Stingy Jack made a pact with Satan. After having tricked the devil, Jack was denied entrance into either Heaven or Hell. As he was banished to eternal darkness, he was given an ember to light his way. In Ireland, Scotland and Wales, on All Hallows Eve children carried an ember in a hollowed-out turnip. In the New World it was found that a pumpkin made a splendid alternative to the turnip. Today the only jack-o'-lanterns carried door to door

are plastic, but the traditional candle-lit jack-o'-lantern graces many a doorstep or window where trick-or-treaters are welcomed.

Marching through the ages the bright orange gourd has continued to appear with regularity. Children of the early 1900s loved L. Frank Baum's classic Land of Oz stories that featured an endearing Jack Pumpkinhead, while present-day children relate to Charlie Brown and Linus waiting for the appearance of the gift-giving 'Great Pumpkin.' The pumpkin continues to have a commercial impact in pop culture with 'Pumpkinhead' horror movies, numerous Pumpkinhead bands and a Pumpkinhead rap song.

It was the celebration of the pumpkin and its association with autumn festivals that tweaked our interest and inspired this book. Ontario's Waterford Pumpkin Fest and long-running Port Elgin Pumpkin Fest are but two examples of events bringing this gourd to national attention. Our local month-long Annapolis Valley Pumpkin Fest further intrigued us because in this celebration, restaurateurs in two adjoining counties have collaborated to create pumpkin-inspired culinary treats. They willingly shared their recipes featuring pumpkin and winter squash, thus providing the base for an innovative array of culinary delights. From breakfast treats to savoury entrées to delectable desserts, we are sure you will find recipes to tempt your palate.

Pumpkin & Squash Varieties

We are highlighting the most popular squash types available to Canadian consumers. There are many varieties under each type; that kind of detail is more significant to the grower than the consumer. For instance, Hubbard Squash may be named True Hubbard, Blue Hubbard, Golden Hubbard, Baby Hubbard, Warted Hubbard and more.

Green Acorn Squash
Small baking squash up to 6 in (15 cm) in length, acorn-shaped. Unique shape makes it excellent for stuffing and attractive for presentation.

Buttercup Squash
Medium to large squash, dark green with narrow grey stripes. Sweet nutty orange flesh with a dense consistency. An all-purpose squash that is good in baked goods and casseroles or as a side dish. May be baked, boiled or steamed.

Butternut Squash
Medium to large squash, also known as the 'pumpkin squash.' A high-yielding pear-shaped, tan-coloured squash with a small seed cavity. An all-purpose squash suitable for baked goods and soups or as a side dish. May be baked, boiled or steamed.

Hubbard Squash
Medium to extra-large squash, dark green, grayish blue to golden in colour. Flesh is fine-grained; best baked or boiled and used as a side dish.

Kabocha Squash
Medium squash with a spotted or blotchy dark green skin. An ideal substitute in pumpkin or sweet potato recipes, the Kabocha is rich and sweet-flavoured. Can be steamed or baked.

Pumpkin
Very small to gigantic (over 1000 lbs/500 kg). Skin ranges in colour from deep orange to blond and flesh is orange. Small pumpkins are primarily used for baking while large ones are more suited to ornamental purposes, such as jack-o'-lanterns for Hallowe'en and Thanksgiving decorations. Large commercial industry processes pumpkin into purée for baked goods.

Red Kuri Squash
Medium-sized, thick-skinned squash, reddish-orange in colour. Originating in Japan, the flesh is delicate with a chestnut flavour. Good for baking and steaming; purées well.

Spaghetti Squash
Medium-sized, smooth-skinned yellow squash. When cooked the flesh forms translucent spaghetti-like strands that are mild in flavour. Usually baked, but can be boiled or steamed.

Turban Squash
Small to medium-sized with a multi-coloured turban-like top. Frequently used as a decorative table piece. Flesh has a delicate nutty flavour; good baked or steamed.

Pumpkin Cream Cheese Muffins, p.20

Breakfast

It is often said that breakfast is the most important meal of the day. With this collection of recipes you are sure to find something to get the day off to a great start.

Pumpkin Cream Cheese
French Toast

Keltic Lodge, Ingonish Beach, NS

Dale Nichols, executive chef at Keltic Lodge, makes this special French toast with a spiced pumpkin and cream cheese filling stuffed between slices of sweet brioche bread, sautéed until golden brown and then finished with maple syrup and icing sugar … you will be hopping out of bed in anticipation!

If you are unable to find brioche by the loaf, feel free to substitute challah bread or any other good-quality white bread.

½ cup (125 mL) pumpkin purée
¾ cup (175 mL) cream cheese
½ tsp (2 mL) ground cinnamon
¼ tsp (1 mL) ground ginger
pinch ground nutmeg
pinch ground allspice
2 tbsp (30 mL) granulated sugar
8 eggs
⅔ cup (150 mL) milk (3.25% m.f.)
1 loaf brioche bread, ends removed, cut in ½-in
  (1-cm) slices
butter for sautéing
pure maple syrup
icing sugar

In a food processor, combine pumpkin, cream cheese, spices, and sugar; pulse until smooth. Remove to a bowl and refrigerate.

In a large bowl, whisk eggs and milk together until frothy. Spread pumpkin mixture on one slice of bread, leaving a ¼-in (5-mm) edge. Top with a second slice of bread and press lightly to adhere. Repeat with remaining bread. Carefully dip breads into egg mixture, letting them fully absorb the liquid.

Heat butter in a skillet to 375°F (190°C). Add breads and sauté on one side until golden, flip and continue sautéing until egg is cooked through, about 8 to 10 minutes.

To serve: place toasts on warmed plates, top with maple syrup, and dust with icing sugar.

Serves 6.

Pumpkin Cranberry
Muffins

Jakobstettel Inn, St. Jacobs, ON

Plan on baking these moist muffins often because they are sure to become a breakfast favourite. Better still, double the recipe and freeze half for future enjoyment.

2 eggs
1 cup (250 mL) granulated sugar
¾ cup + 2 tbsp (210 mL) pumpkin purée
¾ cup (175 mL) vegetable oil
1 ½ cups (375 mL) all-purpose flour
½ tbsp (7 mL) ground cinnamon
1 tsp (5 mL) baking powder
1 tsp (5 mL) baking soda
½ tsp (2 mL) salt
1 cup (250 mL) dried cranberries

Preheat oven to 375°F (190°C). Prepare muffin tin.

In a large mixing bowl, whisk together the eggs and sugar. Slowly beat in pumpkin and oil. Add flour, cinnamon, baking powder, baking soda, and salt; mix until smooth. Stir in cranberries.

Spoon into muffin cups, filling two-thirds full. Bake 15 to 20 minutes or until a toothpick inserted in the centre comes out clean.

Makes 12 muffins.

Golden Pancakes
with Orange Maple Syrup

Just like a sun-filled morning — these pancakes will leave you smiling and begging for them another day. They are easy to prepare and simply delicious.

1 ½ cups (375 mL) all-purpose flour
1 ½ tsp (7 mL) baking powder
½ tsp (2 mL) baking soda
½ tsp (2 mL) salt
2 tbsp (30 mL) granulated sugar
pinch ground nutmeg
pinch ground cloves
½ tsp (2 mL) ground cinnamon
1 ¾ cups (425 mL) buttermilk
½ cup (125 mL) pumpkin purée
1 whole egg + 1 egg white
2 tbsp (30 mL) vegetable oil
additional vegetable oil for cooking
Orange Maple Syrup (recipe follows)

In a large bowl, sift together dry ingredients.

In another bowl, beat buttermilk, pumpkin, egg, and oil until smooth. Add liquid to dry ingredients, stirring until just blended. (Some lumps will remain.)

Heat griddle to medium-high and coat with vegetable oil. Dollop the batter, ¼ cup (60 mL) at a time, on hot skillet. Cook pancakes until surface begins to bubble; turn and bake until golden. Remove pancakes and keep warm. Repeat cooking procedure with remaining batter.

To serve: arrange pancakes on warmed plates. Top with butter and warm Orange Maple Syrup.

Makes about 14 pancakes.

Orange Maple Syrup:
1 cup (250 mL) pure maple syrup
zest of 1 orange

In a small saucepan, combine syrup and orange zest. Over low heat, gently heat and steep, being careful not to boil.

Makes 1 cup (250 mL).

Pumpkin
Cream Cheese Muffins

Evangeline Inn and Café, Grand Pré, NS

These little muffins with their surprise filling will delight both young and old.

1 egg, beaten
½ cup (125 mL) milk
½ cup (125 mL) pumpkin purée
⅓ cup (75 mL) vegetable oil
1 ¾ cups (425 mL) all-purpose flour
½ cup (125 mL) granulated sugar
1 tbsp (15 mL) baking powder
½ tsp (2 mL) ground cinnamon
½ tsp (2 mL) ground nutmeg
¼ tsp (1 mL) ground ginger
¼ tsp (1 mL) salt
4 oz (125 g) cream cheese

Topping:
¼ cup (60 mL) brown sugar
½ tsp (2 mL) ground cinnamon
1 tbsp (15 mL) butter

Preheat oven to 400°F (200°C). Grease muffin tins or line with paper baking cups.

Whisk together the egg, milk, pumpkin, and oil in a large bowl. In a separate bowl combine the flour, sugar, baking powder, spices, and salt. Slowly add dry ingredients to egg mixture, stirring until fully incorporated. In a small bowl rub together brown sugar, cinnamon, and butter to form a topping.

Fill muffin tins half full. Divide cream cheese into 12 equal pieces and place one piece on batter in each cup. Top with remaining batter and sprinkle with topping. Bake until cooked, about 20 minutes.

Makes 12 muffins.

Pumpkin Buttermilk
Biscuits

Traditional buttermilk biscuits have been a mainstay in North American kitchens for generations. These delicious yellow biscuits offer an updated version of the original recipe and are sure to become a frequent addition to your table.

To make a savoury biscuit, add 1 tsp (5 mL) dried herb of choice (thyme, basil, etc.) to the dry ingredients.

2 cups (500 mL) all-purpose flour
½ tsp (2 mL) salt
2 ½ tsp (12 mL) baking powder
½ tsp (2 mL) baking soda
1 ½ tbsp (22 mL) granulated sugar
5 tbsp (75 mL) butter, cubed
¾ cup (175 mL) buttermilk
½ cup (125 mL) pumpkin purée

Preheat oven to 425°F (220°C). Lightly grease a baking sheet.

Combine flour, salt, baking powder, soda, and sugar in a large bowl. Add butter and mix with fingertips until crumbly. In a bowl, whisk buttermilk and pumpkin until smooth. Make a well in dry ingredients and add liquid; stir with a fork until just combined.

Transfer to a floured surface, knead 4 to 5 times and pat out 1 in (2.5 cm) thick. Using a 2 ½-in (6-cm) cookie-cutter, cut out rounds. Do not overwork the dough, as the biscuits will toughen.

Arrange biscuits on baking sheet and bake for about 12 minutes. Transfer to a wire rack to cool.

Makes 1 dozen.

Pumpkin
Bread

Sunset on the River Bed & Breakfast, Upper Kingsclear, NB

Judy Spink, proprietor of Sunset on the River, frequently serves this delicious sweet, spicy loaf for breakfast.

This recipe makes 2 loaves of sweet bread. We recommend one loaf for immediate use; store the other in the freezer, for up to one month.

3 cups (750 mL) all-purpose flour
2 tsp (10 mL) baking powder
2 tsp (10 mL) baking soda
1 tsp (5 mL) salt
1 tbsp (15 mL) ground cinnamon
2 cups (500 mL) granulated sugar
4 eggs
1 ¼ cup (310 mL) vegetable oil
2 ½ cups (625 mL) pumpkin purée
½ cup (125 mL) chopped walnuts
⅓ cup (75 mL) raisins
icing sugar (optional)

Preheat oven to 350°F (180°C). Grease two 9 x 5-in (22.5 x 12.5-cm) loaf pans.

Sift together flour, baking powder, soda, salt, and cinnamon. In a mixer, combine sugar, eggs, and oil; beat until smooth. With mixer on low speed, add pumpkin purée alternately with flour mixture; mix until well combined. Stir in walnuts and raisins.

Divide batter between the two loaf pans. Let stand 10 minutes then bake until a toothpick inserted in the centre of the loaf comes out clean, about 50 to 60 minutes. Cool on a rack before removing from pans.

Dust top with icing sugar if desired.

Makes 2 loaves.

Healthy Autumn
Granola

Unlike purchasing commercial cereal products, when making your own cereal you alone control the ingredients for quality and content. Use unsaturated fats, pure sugars, and your favourite dried fruits, nuts, and grains. Presto — you have created your own nutritious breakfast.

Serve with milk or soy milk, over yoghurt, or by the 'handful' as a trail mix. This granola also works well as a topping for apple or other fruit crisps.

5 cups (1.25 L) rolled oats
1 cup (250 mL) oat bran
¼ cup (60 mL) wheat germ
½ cup (125 mL) ground flax seeds*
1 ½ cups (375 mL) sliced almonds
1 cup (250 mL) pecan pieces
1 ⅓ cups (325 mL) shelled sunflower seeds
1 ½ cups (375 mL) shelled pumpkin seeds
½ cup (125 mL) vegetable oil
2 cups (500 mL) raisins
1 cup (250 mL) dried cranberries
2 cups (500 mL) mixed dried fruit of choice
   (apricots, dates, apple, pear, mango, etc.),
   chopped
½ cup (125 mL) liquid honey
1 tbsp (15 mL) vegetable oil (2nd amount)
1 tsp (5 mL) vanilla

Place oven racks in upper and lower thirds of the oven and preheat to 325°F (160°C).

In a large bowl, combine oats, oat bran, wheat germ, flax seeds, almonds, pecans, sunflower seeds, and pumpkin seeds. Add vegetable oil and stir to coat. Spread on two rimmed baking sheets and bake 30 minutes, stirring every 10 minutes. After 2nd stirring, switch rack position of baking sheets. Transfer to a large bowl and stir in raisins, cranberries, and mixed dried fruit.

In a bowl, combine honey, oil (2nd amount), and vanilla and lightly heat in microwave. Pour honey mixture over granola and stir to combine.

Spread granola on baking sheets; return to oven and bake until lightly golden, about 10 minutes. Remove from oven and let cool completely before storing in airtight containers.

This granola will keep at room temperature for up to 2 weeks; it may also be frozen.

Makes about 5 lb (2.5 kg), or 40 servings.

*Grind flax seeds in a coffee grinder, blender or food processor. Unlike whole flax seeds which pass directly through the digestive system, ground flax seeds will release their nutritional goodness in the digestive process.

Acadian
Pumpkin Jam

Sunset on the River Bed & Breakfast, Upper Kingsclear, NB

Our Acadian ancestors knew what to do when faced with the annual pumpkin harvest 'overload'. They turned the lovely orange vegetable into a marmalade-style jam, bringing colour and spicy flavour to the breakfast table throughout the year.

Judy Spink tells us that, if you prefer, you can substitute an orange for the lemon in the recipe.

12 cups (3 L) peeled, seeded, and cubed
    pumpkin (½-in (1-cm) cubes)
6 cups (1.5 L) granulated sugar
1 large lemon
15 whole cloves

In a large bowl, combine pumpkin and sugar; stir to mix well. Cover with a plate, weight well, and let stand overnight, or at least 15 hours. Remove pumpkin mixture to a large stockpot.

Thinly slice lemon (do not peel) and coarsely chop; discard seeds. Tie cloves in a cheesecloth bag.

Add pumpkin, lemon, and cloves to stockpot and mix well to combine. Bring to a boil over medium heat. Cook, stirring occasionally, until juice is the consistency of medium syrup and the pumpkin is translucent, about 30 minutes.

Discard cloves. Ladle jam into sterilized jars and seal. Cover, cool, and store.

Makes six 8-oz (250-mL) jars.

Baked Sugar Pears with Pumpkin, Blue Ermite Cheese, and Toasted Walnut Stuffing, p.34

First Course

The first course or appetizer sets the tone of your dinner. In this collection we offer several unique soup recipes, seasonal salads, and an unusual preparation for a whole baked pumpkin. We know these dishes will provide a great beginning to your meal.

Farmers' Harvest
Salad

The Old Orchard Inn, Greenwich, NS

Pumpkin seeds, also called pepitas, are easy to dry and shell, or you can purchase them in the bulk food sections of many markets. Used as a crunchy garnish to many dishes, their health benefits include being a very good source of magnesium and phosphorus. The chef notes that he often serves this salad with a grilled chicken breast and a sprinkling of blue cheese.

Caramelized Pumpkin (recipe follows)
Salad Dressing (recipe follows)
1 English cucumber
mesclun mix to serve four
1 large apple, cored
1 pear, cored
juice of 1 lemon
2 tbsp (30 mL) shelled pumpkin seeds, as
   garnish

Prepare Caramelized Pumpkin and Salad Dressing and set aside.

Rinse cucumber and pat dry. Cut off ends and slice lengthwise in approximately ¼-in (5-mm) slices. Take four inner slices of cucumber and form into rings. Place one ring on each of four chilled salad plates and fill with greens so that they resemble a bouquet.

Thinly slice apple and pear, and brush with lemon juice to avoid discolouration. Arrange fruit slices on sides of plates and sprinkle entire salad with caramelized pumpkin and pumpkin seeds. Drizzle with salad dressing.

Serves 4.

Caramelized Pumpkin:
1 ½ cups (375 mL) pumpkin in ½-in (1-cm) dice
¼ cup (60 mL) pure maple syrup

Preheat oven to 350°F (180°C). Toss prepared pumpkin with maple syrup and bake until tender and caramelized, about 15 minutes. Set aside to cool. Makes 1 ½ cups (375 mL).

Salad Dressing:
1 tbsp (15 mL) Dijon mustard
¼ cup (60 mL) apple cider vinegar
½ cup (125 mL) Caramelized Pumpkin
1 small garlic clove, minced
½ cup (125 mL) olive oil
salt and pepper

Using a food processor, combine mustard, vinegar, pumpkin and garlic. With motor running, slowly pour in oil and process until emulsified. Season to taste with salt and pepper.

Autumn Greens
with Raspberry Vinaigrette and
Toasted Pumpkin Seeds

Bishop's Restaurant, Vancouver, BC

Salad greens grow best in the cool weather of early autumn when daytime temperatures lower. Executive chef Dennis Green finds that these autumn greens tossed with a simple raspberry vinaigrette and toasted pumpkin seeds make a wonderful crunchy salad.

1 shallot, sliced
½ tsp (2 mL) Dijon mustard
¼ cup (60 mL) raspberry vinegar
½ cup (125 mL) grape seed oil (or walnut or
    hazelnut oil)
¼ cup (60 mL) vegetable oil
salt and freshly ground pepper
6 to 8 cups (1.5 to 2 L) mixed autumn salad
    greens (any combination of arugula, curly
    endive, chicory, baby romaine, chervil, etc.)
¾ cup (175 mL) toasted, shelled pumpkin seeds*

In a blender or food processor, process shallot, mustard, and vinegar until smooth. With motor running, slowly add oils. Season vinaigrette with salt and pepper.

To serve: toss greens with desired amount of vinaigrette, then arrange on chilled plates. Garnish with toasted pumpkin seeds.

Serves 6.

*To toast pumpkin seeds:
Preheat oven to 400°F (200°C). Arrange seeds on a baking sheet and bake, stirring frequently, until fragrant and lightly toasted, about 5 to 6 minutes.

Baked Sugar Pears with
Pumpkin, Blue Ermite Cheese, and Toasted Walnut Stuffing

Peller Estates Winery Restaurant, Niagara-on-the-Lake, ON

An ideal recipe for entertaining — you can prepare the pears and dressing early in the day and reheat the pears a few minutes before serving. Executive chef Jason Parsons uses the dainty and super-sweet Seckel pear, also known as 'sugar pear', in this recipe. If it is unavailable you may substitute Anjou, Bartlett, or Bosc pears but they will be larger and require a longer cooking time.

Blue Ermite cheese is a sharp crumbly Canadian blue cheese similar to Danish blue cheese.

6 sugar pears
2 tbsp (30 mL) melted butter
1 tbsp (15 mL) liquid honey
½ cup (125 mL) pumpkin, finely diced
1 tbsp (15 mL) brown sugar
1 tbsp (15 mL) butter, softened
3 tbsp (45 mL) Blue Ermite cheese, crumbled
⅔ cup (150 mL) walnut halves, toasted *
3 Belgian endives, divided into spears
mâche or mixed greens to serve 6
Blue Cheese Dressing (recipe follows)

Preheat oven to 350°F (180°C).

Arrange pears upright in a baking dish. Drizzle 1 tsp (5 mL) melted butter and ½ tsp (2 mL) honey on each. Bake in oven until cooked, about 20 minutes. Cool and reserve.

In a bowl, toss pumpkin with brown sugar and butter. Spread on a baking sheet and bake until caramelized, about 20 minutes, stirring once or twice. Cool and reserve.

Toast walnuts then cool. Chop 6 tbsp (90 mL) for stuffing; reserve remaining walnut halves for garnish. In a small bowl, combine pumpkin, cheese, and chopped walnuts for stuffing.

Preheat oven to 425°F (220°C).

Slice tops off pears and scoop out cores with a melon baller. Fill pear cavities with pumpkin mixture and cover with tops. Reheat pears until warmed through, about 5 minutes.

To serve: arrange mixed greens in centre of 6 large dinner plates, position endive spears in a 'spoke fashion' around greens, and place walnut halves between spokes. Centre pears on greens and drizzle with Blue Cheese Dressing.

Serves 6.

*To toast walnuts: preheat oven to 350°F (180°C). Sprinkle nuts in a single layer on a baking sheet and bake until golden brown, about 6 minutes. Stir once or twice during toasting to aid even browning.

Blue Cheese Dressing:
½ cup (125 mL) apple cider
1 whole star anise
2 whole cloves
1 small bay leaf
1 cup (250 mL) heavy cream (35% m.f.)
1 ½ tbsp (22 mL) blue cheese

Combine apple cider, star anise, cloves, and bay leaf in a heavy saucepan and reduce over medium heat to 3 tbsp (45 mL). Add cream and continue to reduce by one-half. Remove spices and stir in blue cheese. Cool. If dressing is too thick at serving time thin with a little hot water.

Makes ⅔ cup (150 mL).

Curried Butternut Squash
and Cauliflower Soup

Scanway Catering, Halifax, NS

'A heavenly taste as smooth as velvet' perfectly describes this creamy soup from well-known Halifax chef and restaurateur Unni Simensen.

2 tbsp (30 mL) butter
2 cups (500 mL) chopped onion
1 tbsp (15 mL) curry powder
½ tsp (2 mL) ground cinnamon
salt and pepper
2 tsp (10 mL) liquid honey
5 cups (1.25 L) vegetable stock (or chicken stock)
2 ½ to 3 lb (1.25 to1.5 kg) butternut squash, peeled, seeded and cut in ½-in (1-cm) dice
½ large or 1 medium cauliflower, cut into florets
⅔ cup (150 mL) heavy cream (35% m.f.)
liquid honey, for garnish
fresh thyme sprigs, for garnish

Melt butter in a large saucepan over medium-low heat. Sauté onion until soft, stirring frequently, about 7 minutes. Add curry powder, cinnamon, salt, pepper, and honey, and stir to combine. Add stock, pumpkin, and cauliflower; bring to a boil, reduce heat, cover, and simmer until vegetables are soft, about 20 minutes.

In a blender, purée soup in batches until smooth and creamy. Return soup to saucepan and stir in cream. Adjust seasoning and heat to serving temperature.

To serve: ladle into warmed soup bowls and garnish with a drizzling of liquid honey and a sprig of fresh thyme.

Serves 6 to 8.

Butternut Squash Soup
with Sautéed Québec Foie Gras

Restaurant Les Fougères, Chelsea, QC

Butternut squash, which is sometimes called pumpkin squash, is a popular choice among chefs. Its dense, deep-yellow flesh is very flavourful, and because of its elongated shape and small seed pocket a butternut will provide more vegetable than other squash or pumpkin species.

2 butternut squash, about 2 lbs (1 kg) each
4 oz (125 g) butter
2 tbsp (30 mL) olive oil
2 onions, peeled and chopped
2 stalks celery, chopped
2 medium potatoes, peeled and chopped
3 cups (750 mL) chicken or vegetable stock
1 cup (250 mL) apple cider
½ cup (125 mL) sherry
½ cup (125 mL) pure maple syrup
salt and pepper, to taste
6 oz (185 g) foie gras
all-purpose flour, for dusting
balsamic vinegar, as garnish
fleur de sel,* as garnish

Preheat oven to 375°F (190°C).

Halve squash and place, cut side down, on a foil-lined baking sheet. Bake until tender, about 1 hour. Remove from oven, cool, and discard seeds. Spoon flesh out of squash and reserve.

Heat olive oil and butter in a large saucepan over low heat; sweat onions and celery until translucent. Add reserved squash, chopped potatoes, stock, and cider. Bring to a boil, then reduce heat and simmer until vegetables are tender, about 20 minutes. Stir in sherry and maple syrup, and continue to simmer for another 10 minutes. Cool slightly then process, in batches, in a blender. Season with salt and pepper and return to serving temperature.

Slice chilled foie gras into 6 equal portions. Dust lightly with flour that has been seasoned with salt and pepper. Heat a skillet to searing temperature and sear foie gras about 10 seconds per side. Ladle soup into six bowls and garnish with a piece of foie gras, a drizzle of balsamic vinegar, and a sprinkle of fleur de sel.

Serves 6.

*Fleur de sel (flower of salt) is a premier condiment sea salt harvested in the Guérande region of France's Brittany coast.

Squash Soup
with Bay of Fundy Dulse
and Smoked Salmon

San Martello Dining Room at the Dufferin Inn,
Saint John, NB

The Dufferin Inn's close proximity to the Bay of
Fundy allows chef and owner Axel Begner to
innovatively incorporate local ingredients into his
menu. Dulse is dried red seaweed, which is
harvested along the Fundy shores.

1 tbsp (15 mL) brown sugar
¼ tsp (1 mL) cayenne pepper
½ tsp (2 mL) salt
1 tbsp (15 mL) olive oil
3 cups (750 mL) peeled, cubed butternut squash
   (2-in (5-cm) cubes)
2 cups (500 mL) chicken or vegetable stock
1 tbsp (15 mL) butter
2 tbsp (30 mL) dulse flakes
2 oz (60 g) cold-smoked salmon, julienned,
   as garnish

Preheat oven to 375°F (190°C).

In a small bowl combine brown sugar, cayenne
pepper, salt, and olive oil. Place squash cubes on
a rimmed baking sheet and sprinkle with sugar
mixture. Bake, turning occasionally, until tender
and browned, about 40 minutes. Transfer to a
food processor and purée.

Transfer squash to a saucepan and stir in stock.
Reheat to serving temperature. Melt butter in a
skillet and add dulse flakes; sauté until crisp.
Serve soup sprinkled with dulse and garnished
with smoked salmon.

Serves 4.

Maple Roasted Pumpkin
and Pear Soup

Art Can Gallery, Canning, NS

We have found many recipes that combine pumpkins with pears and we continue to be amazed at how they complement each other. At the Gallery the chef prepares his soup using heavy cream. It may also be prepared with blend (10% m.f.), without compromising the flavour. Garnish this slightly sweet soup with toasted pumpkin seeds.

¼ small baking pumpkin, peeled and sliced
   (about ½ lb/250 g)
2 tbsp (30 mL) pure maple syrup, divided
1 tbsp (15 mL) brown sugar
1 small onion, diced
1 large clove garlic, minced
1 tbsp (15 mL) vegetable oil
1 tbsp (15 mL) white wine
6 cups (1.5 L) apple juice
¼ cup (60 mL) water
2 pears, peeled and diced
¼ tsp (1 mL) ground nutmeg
⅛ tsp (.5 mL) ground ginger
1 tsp (5 mL) dried oregano
2 cups (500 mL) heavy cream (35% m.f.)
salt and pepper
Toasted Pumpkin Seeds (recipe follows)

Preheat oven to 350°F (180°C).

Peel and slice pumpkin, reserving seeds, and place on a foil-lined baking sheet. Sprinkle with 1 tbsp (15 mL) maple syrup and brown sugar. Bake until pumpkin is soft, about 30 minutes. Set aside.

In a large saucepan, sauté onion and garlic in oil until translucent, about five minutes. Stir frequently, being careful not to allow vegetables to brown. Deglaze pan with white wine. Add apple juice, water, diced pears, spices, remaining maple syrup, pumpkin, and cream. Bring to a boil then immediately reduce heat; simmer until pears are tender. Cool slightly and purée in batches with a food processor or blender; return to serving temperature. Season to taste with salt and pepper and serve garnished with toasted pumpkin seeds.

Serves 4 to 6.

Toasted Pumpkin Seeds:

Pumpkin seeds may be eaten either shelled or whole; the shells are edible and are a good source of fibre.

1 cup (250 mL) fresh pumpkin seeds
2 tsp (10 mL) peanut oil
2 tsp (10 mL) melted butter
salt

Wipe pumpkin seeds, being careful to remove all pulp. Set aside for several hours to dry. Toss seeds with oil and melted butter to coat, and season with salt. Spread on a baking sheet and roast at 350°F (180°C), stirring often, until crisp and golden, about 30 minutes. Cool.

Split Pea
and Pumpkin Soup

Fireside Café, Canning, NS

'Spicy with a touch of sweetness' best describes this hearty soup from the Fireside kitchen. It is easily a meal in itself when accompanied by freshly baked bread and a wedge of your favourite cheese.

1 cup (250 mL) yellow split peas
4 cups (1 L) water
2 stalks celery, chopped
½ Spanish onion, chopped
2 cups (500 mL) diced pumpkin (or squash of choice)
1 ½ cups (375 mL) diced tomatoes (canned or fresh)
1 cup (250 mL) puréed pumpkin
1 ½ tsp (7 mL) tarragon leaves
½ tsp (2 mL) ground mace
½ tsp (2 mL) ground cumin
1 ½ tsp (7 mL) chili powder
½ tsp (2 mL) ground coriander
2 tbsp (30 mL) brown sugar
salt and pepper

In a sieve, rinse split peas until water runs clear. In a large stockpot combine split peas and water, and soak overnight.

Add celery, onion, and diced pumpkin to stockpot ingredients. Bring to a boil; reduce heat, cover, and simmer until peas are totally softened, stirring frequently. (This may take 2 to 3 hours.)

Add tomatoes, puréed pumpkin, spices, and brown sugar to stockpot; bring back to simmer and cook 30 minutes. If necessary, add additional water to reach desired thickness. Adjust seasoning with salt and pepper to taste.

Serves 6.

Pumpkin Coconut
Bisque

Paddy's Pub, Kentville, NS

The creation of chef Daniel Mons, this bisque will appeal to lovers of Thai cuisine. Coconut milk is found in cans in the international food section of most supermarkets. It should not be confused with "cream of coconut" or "coconut cream," which are sweetened and used for desserts or drinks.

1 tbsp (15 mL) butter
½ cup (125 mL) chopped onion
1 clove garlic, minced
2 cups (500 mL) puréed pumpkin
1 ¼ cups (300 mL) chicken broth
1 tbsp (15 mL) granulated sugar
¼ tsp (1 mL) allspice
¼ tsp (1 mL) crushed chili peppers
1 cup (250 mL) coconut milk
salt and pepper, to taste
½ cup (125 mL) shredded coconut, toasted,* as
    garnish (optional)

Melt butter over medium heat in a heavy saucepan; sauté onion and garlic until softened and starting to take on colour. Stir in pumpkin, broth, sugar, allspice, chili peppers, and coconut milk. Bring to a boil, reduce heat, and simmer, covered, 20 minutes.

Cool slightly, then purée in batches in a blender. Return to saucepan, adjust seasoning with salt and pepper, and bring back to serving temperature. Serve garnished with a sprinkling of toasted coconut.

Serves 4.

*To toast coconut: spread coconut on a baking sheet and toast in a 350°F (180°C) oven for 5 minutes or until lightly browned. Remove to a plate to cool.

Roasted Butternut
Squash Soup

Arbor View Inn, Lunenburg, NS

Chef Daniel Orovec chooses Annapolis Valley McIntosh apples for his creamy soup, although any sweet-flavoured apple variety may be used. He notes that the dish may be garnished with snipped chives and freshly diced apple.

2 lb (1 kg) butternut squash
1 tbsp (15 mL) vegetable oil
2 tbsp (30 mL) butter
1 medium onion, chopped
2 stalks celery, chopped
2 large McIntosh apples, peeled and diced
3 ½ cups (875 mL) vegetable stock
salt and pepper, to taste
½ cup (125 mL) heavy cream (35% m.f.)

Preheat oven to 400°F (200°C).

Halve squash, remove seeds, and brush flesh with oil. Bake 40 minutes or until squash is tender and slightly caramelized on top. Remove from oven, cool slightly, peel, and cut in cubes.

In a heavy-bottomed pan over medium heat, melt butter and gently sauté onion and celery until onion is translucent. Add squash and sauté 2 minutes to allow flavours to combine. Add apples and stock, cover saucepan, and simmer 20 minutes. Purée soup, in batches, in a food processor or blender. Return to saucepan, season to taste with salt and pepper, and stir in cream. Return to serving temperature.

Serves 6.

Baked Stuffed
Pumpkin

This appetizer presents well and makes a great conversation piece. A steaming, golden pumpkin stuffed with herbed bread and cheese and arranged on a bed of bright greens … Wow!

It is easy to turn this recipe into a luncheon or main course entrée by adding 1 cup (250 mL) of browned sausage or chorizo to the bread mixture. Serve with a green salad and fresh crusty rolls.

1 baking pumpkin (2 to 4 lb/1 to 2 kg)
olive oil
salt
3 tbsp (45 mL) butter
1 small onion, chopped
½ cup (125 mL) chopped celery
4 cups (1 L) day-old bread in ¼ in (1-cm) cubes
1 ½ tsp (7 mL) dried Italian herbs, crushed
salt and pepper
1 cup (250 mL) shredded Swiss cheese
1 cup (250 mL) shredded cheddar cheese
3 eggs
1 cup (250 mL) blend (10% m.f.)
1 bay leaf
leafy greens, for garnish

Wash and dry pumpkin. Cut a lid about 4 in (10 cm) in diameter out of the top of the pumpkin. Scrape and remove seeds and all stringy material from pumpkin.

Heat butter in a skillet over medium heat; add onion and celery and sauté until soft. Add the bread cubes, herbs, salt, and pepper; toss to combine. Remove from heat and stir in the cheeses. Rub inside of pumpkin with olive oil and sprinkle lightly with salt. Spoon the cheese mixture into the pumpkin.

Preheat oven to 400° F (200° C). In a bowl, whisk together eggs and blend. Pour egg mixture into the pumpkin. Lay bay leaf on top, replace the lid and place in a greased baking dish. Bake for 1 to 1 ½ hours or until pumpkin begins to soften and inside starts to bubble (baking time will depend on size of pumpkin). Reduce heat to 350°F (180°C) and bake an additional 30 minutes or until pumpkin meat is tender.

To serve: place on a large platter garnished with leafy greens accompanied with dipping crackers, pita triangles, or corn chips.

*Seared Sea Scallops on Butternut Squash and
Potato Pavé with Basil Oil, p.56*

Entrées

We were pleasantly surprised with the variety of pumpkin and squash entrée recipes submitted by Canadian chefs from coast to coast. Pumpkin and squash complement meat dishes beautifully, and are equally delicious with seafood ingredients.

Grilled Strip Loin
with Butternut Squash,
Cumin and Lime Condiment

Keltic Lodge, Ingonish Beach, NS

It is a tradition in Atlantic Canada to accompany meals with condiments. No meal is complete without some form of pickle, mustard, or sauce, be it savoury or sweet. Dale Nichols, executive chef at Keltic Lodge, loves to experiment with this tradition by preparing special accompaniments with seasonal ingredients. He comments that this condiment also pairs well with halibut and salmon.

Condiment:

¼ cup (60 mL) canola oil, portioned
2 cups (500 mL) diced red onion
1 ½ lb (750 g) butternut squash (or squash of
    choice), peeled and finely diced
1 tbsp (15 mL) minced garlic
2 tbsp (30 mL) ground cumin
½ cup (125 mL) water
¼ cup (60 mL) molasses
¼ cup (60 mL) fresh orange juice
¼ cup (60 mL) red wine vinegar
2 limes, cut in half
½ cup (125 mL) roughly chopped parsley

Heat 2 tbsp (30 mL) oil in a large saucepan over medium heat; add onion and sauté, stirring occasionally, until translucent, about 6 minutes.

Remove onion from pan and reserve.

Return saucepan to heat; add remaining oil and heat until hot but not smoking. Add squash and sauté, stirring occasionally, until browned, about 5 minutes. Add reserved onion to pan along with garlic and cumin. Sauté, stirring frequently, for 1 minute. Add water, molasses, orange juice, and vinegar; bring to a simmer. Cook, lightly covered and stirring occasionally, until squash is tender but not overcooked, about 10 minutes.

Remove squash from heat; squeeze lime juice on mixture, sprinkle with parsley, and stir to combine. Cover and keep warm while preparing the steaks.

Steaks:

6 strip loin steaks, 1 in (2.5cm) thick
¼ cup (60 mL) mixed peppercorns, crushed

Heat a grill or barbecue. Season steaks with a generous coating of crushed peppercorns. Cook steaks on a hot barbecue or grill, turning once during the cooking — about 5 minutes for rare, 8 minutes for medium, and 12 minutes for well-done.

To serve: arrange steaks on warmed plates, top with condiment, and accompany with additional vegetables of choice.

Serves 6.

Roasted Loin of Pork
on Golden Harvest Sauce

The Old Orchard Inn, Greenwich, NS

The creation of chef Joe Gillis, this succulent sauce utilizes the best of autumn's harvest. He notes that it is equally delicious served with seafood such as grilled salmon.

3 to 4 lb (1.5 to 2 kg) loin of pork, boneless
  and rolled
1 tbsp (15 mL) olive oil
salt and freshly ground black pepper
¾ cup (175 mL) diced pumpkin
¼ cup (60 mL) diced sweet potato
¾ cup (175 mL) diced squash
½ carrot, peeled and chopped
½ onion, peeled and chopped
1 garlic clove, chopped
½ apple, peeled and chopped
1 cup (250 mL) chicken stock
1-in (3-cm) cinnamon stick
1 tsp (5 mL) curry powder, or to taste
1 ½ tsp (7 mL) brown sugar
1 small bay leaf
salt and pepper, to taste

Preheat oven to 450°F (230°C).

Rinse pork loin and pat dry; rub with olive oil, and season with salt and pepper. Roast 10 minutes then reduce heat to 350°F (180°C) and continue to roast, allowing 30 minutes per pound or until the internal temperature of the roast reaches 160°F (70°C). Remove from oven, tent with foil, and let rest for 10 minutes before slicing.

While roast is baking, prepare sauce. Bring remaining ingredients to a boil in a large saucepan over medium-high heat. Reduce heat and simmer, stirring occasionally, until vegetables are fully cooked, about 30 minutes. Purée in a blender, season to taste with salt and pepper, and keep warm.

To serve: arrange pork slices on plates and nap with golden harvest sauce.

Serves 6.

Pork Tenderloin with
Chili-rubbed Pumpkin
Seed Crust

Westover Inn, St. Marys, ON

Pork tenderloins are the easiest meat to prepare and present when entertaining, and the crowning glory is their flavour and tenderness. Tenderloins frequently come in packages of two and we prefer to cook both as this always ensures 'seconds.' Leftover pork tenderloin is delicious in salads or thinly sliced in sandwiches.

2 pork tenderloins, 13 to 18 oz (375 to 500 g) each
sea salt and coarsely ground pepper
2 tbsp (30 mL) olive oil
Ancho Chili Paste (recipe follows)
Toasted Pumpkin Seeds (recipe follows)

Prepare chili paste and toasted seeds, and reserve.

Preheat oven to 400°F (200°C).

Trim fat and silverskin from tenderloins; tuck thin 'tail' end underneath to make a uniform thickness. Generously coat with salt and pepper. In a heavy-bottomed ovenproof skillet, heat oil over medium-high heat; sear tenderloins on all sides, about 5 minutes. Remove from heat and spread a thin layer of the Ancho Chili Paste on one side of each tenderloin.

Spread the pumpkin seed crumbs in an even layer on a large plate. Roll the tenderloins (chili paste side down) in the crumbs and press to adhere.

Return to skillet and bake in oven until internal temperature reaches 160°F (70°C), about 12 to 15 minutes. Remove from oven and let rest for 5 to 10 minutes.

To serve: slice on the diagonal and serve with vegetables of choice.

Serves 6.

Ancho Chili Paste:
6 dried ancho chili peppers
boiling water

Cut tops off and remove seeds from chili peppers. Place in a bowl and cover completely with boiling water. Soak for about 45 minutes and then drain. With a spatula, scrape pulp from skin. Purée pulp in a food processor until smooth.

Toasted Pumpkin Seeds:
1 cup (250 mL) shelled pumpkin seeds

Preheat oven to 400°F (200°C). Spread seeds on a baking sheet and bake, shaking the pan once or twice, until golden and fragrant, about 5 to 6 minutes. (Watch carefully, so as not to burn.) Cool completely.

In a food processor, pulse seeds until crumb-like.

Seared Sea Scallops on
Butternut Squash and Potato
Pavé with Basil Oil

Westin Nova Scotian Hotel, Halifax, NS

Executive chef Mike McKinnon has created a most impressive entrée that successfully balances a variety of different flavours. He offsets the sweetness of the pavé and succulent scallops with a generous portion of peppery watercress. The result is heavenly.

1 ½ lb (750 g) large sea scallops (about 12)
¼ cup (60 mL) olive oil, divided
1 clove garlic, minced
2 tsp (10 mL) minced cilantro
¼ cup (60 mL) white wine
sea salt and coarse ground pepper
watercress for garnish
Butternut Squash and Potato Pavé (recipe follows)
Basil Oil (recipe follows)

Prepare Butternut Squash and Potato Pavé and Basil Oil; reserve.

Rinse scallops, remove the tough small muscle, and pat dry. In a bowl combine 2 tbsp (30 mL) olive oil, garlic, cilantro, salt and pepper; add scallops, cover, and marinate for 30 minutes.

In a large skillet, heat remaining oil on medium-high heat. Remove scallops from marinade and add to skillet. Sear scallops approximately 2 minutes, turning once. Add wine to the pan for the second minute of cooking. Remove scallops and slice each scallop crosswise into 3 medallions.

Preheat oven to 275°F (140°C). Slice pavé into 6 equal portions. Place on a baking sheet and heat for 5 minutes. Arrange scallop medallions in a uniform pattern on top of each portion and return to oven until heated, about 2 to 3 minutes.

To serve: place scallop-topped pavé portions in the centre of 6 dinner plates. Mound a small portion of watercress on top and drizzle with Basil Oil. Drizzle a little more oil around the plate.

Serves 6.

Butternut Squash and Potato Pavé:
A mandolin will slice the squash and potato slices very thin. If you do not own a mandolin, cut the vegetables as thin as possible by hand.
½ lb (250 g) butternut squash, peeled and seeded
2 to 3 Yukon Gold potatoes, peeled
1 clove garlic, minced
¼ cup (60 mL) melted butter
salt and pepper
¼ cup (60 mL) brown sugar
1 cup (250 mL) grated Romano cheese

Preheat oven to 350°F (180°C). Line the bottom of a 10-in (25-cm) cast-iron skillet with parchment paper.

Slice squash and potatoes very thinly.
Add minced garlic to butter and keep warm for easy spreading.

Arrange a layer of potato slices on the bottom of the pan, slightly overlapping each slice. Brush with garlic butter, season with salt and pepper, and sprinkle with cheese. Add a layer of squash slices on top of the potato, brush with garlic butter, season with salt and pepper, and sprinkle first with brown sugar and then cheese. Alternate layers of squash and potato, ending with a potato layer.

Place a second piece of parchment paper over the pavé followed by a sheet of foil; press down firmly. Place a weight (another cast-iron skillet, foil-covered brick, or other heavy weight) on top of the pavé. Bake 45 to 60 minutes until nearly cooked. Remove weight and covering and bake until golden, about 15 minutes. Invert onto a large plate and remove parchment paper; cool.

Basil Oil:

This will keep for up to a week in the refrigerator. Use also as a salad dressing or a marinade for meat, chicken, or fish.

1 cup (250 mL) packed fresh basil leaves
2 tbsp (30 mL) chopped chives
½ cup (125 mL) green leaf lettuce (or spinach)
1 cup (250 mL) olive oil
salt and pepper

Blanch basil, lettuce, and chives in boiling water for 10 seconds. Drain and run under cold water. Shake to remove excess water.

In a blender, combine greens and oil and blend until very smooth. Season with salt and pepper, and strain through a fine sieve.

Makes 1 cup (250 mL).

Venison Medallions
with Five-spice Pumpkin Chutney

The Blue Door Restaurant, Fredericton, NB

Chefs at The Blue Door comment that this chutney makes a great accompaniment to roast meats, especially game. It also works well with poultry and pork. In this recipe we paired the chutney with seared venison medallions to create a delectable entrée.

1 tbsp (15 mL) olive oil
1 red onion, finely diced
2 tbsp (30 mL) minced fresh ginger
1 tbsp (15 mL) Chinese five-spice powder
1 green Thai chili (or jalapeno pepper), seeded and minced
3 cups (750 mL) peeled and finely diced pumpkin
1 each, red and green pepper, finely diced
4 tomatoes, peeled and diced
1 ¼ cups (310 mL) brown sugar
1 ½ cups (375 mL) cider vinegar
½ cup (125 mL) raisins
¼ cup (60 mL) chopped fresh tarragon
6 pieces fresh venison, 5 to 6 oz (150 to 180 g) each
1 to 2 tsp (5 to 10 mL) olive oil

Heat oil in a heavy stockpot over medium-low heat. Add onion, ginger, chili, and five-spice powder; sauté until soft, about 10 minutes, stirring occasionally. Add pumpkin and peppers; raise heat to medium and cook 5 minutes.

Add tomatoes, sugar, vinegar, and raisins; bring to a boil, reduce heat to simmer, cover loosely, and cook until pumpkin is soft and mixture has thickened. Stir in tarragon and cook for an additional 4 minutes.

Transfer chutney to a bowl and cool, uncovered. Cover and refrigerate for 2 hours to allow flavours to blend. Chutney will keep, refrigerated, for up to 1 week or it may be preserved for longer storage (*see note).

In skillet, heat olive oil over high heat; pan-sear venison on both sides until desired degree of doneness. Remove from heat.

To serve: place venison on warmed plates, accompanied by chutney and vegetables of choice.

Serves 6.

*To preserve chutney for longer storage: remove chutney from stove and immediately ladle into sterilized 8-oz (250-mL) jars. Seal jars with lids and put the sealed jars on the rack in a canner or 8 to 10 qt (8 to 10 L) pot. Add enough water to cover the jars by 2 in (5 cm). Bring to a boil, cover, and boil chutney for 10 minutes. Remove jars from the canner and cool on the counter for 12 to 24 hours. Store in a cool, dark place.

Makes 6 8-oz (250-mL) jars.

Thai Pumpkin
Curry

This sweet Thai-style curry is easily adapted to suit both vegetarian and non-vegetarian tastes. Either vegetable or chicken stock can be used, and chicken or shellfish may be added to vary the recipe.

1 can (15 oz/425 g) coconut cream
1 to 3 tsp (5 to 15 mL) red curry paste ('heat' value rises with amount of curry paste used)
2 Kaffir lime leaves,* quartered
1 stalk lemon grass, peeled and bruised
1 cup (250 mL) chicken or vegetable stock
1 tbsp (15 mL) fish sauce
1 to 2 tsp (5 to 10 mL) granulated sugar
2 lb (1 kg) pumpkin or winter squash, peeled, seeded and cut in 1-in (2.5-cm) cubes
1 large potato, peeled and cut in 1-in (2.5-cm) cubes
1 cup (250 mL) fresh or frozen peas
½ lb (250 g) bok choy, cut in 1-in (2.5-cm) slices
2 to 3 tbsp (30 to 45 mL) lime juice
salt
chopped cilantro for garnish

Separate the heavy cream from the top of the can of coconut cream. Blend this cream with the curry paste in a stockpot over medium heat. Stir in lime leaves, lemon grass, remaining coconut cream, stock, fish sauce, and sugar; bring to a simmer. If necessary, adjust seasoning with more sugar to balance the saltiness of the fish sauce.

Add pumpkin and potato, and cook 10 minutes. Add peas and bok choy, and cook until pumpkin and potato are tender, about 5 minutes. Add lime juice and salt to taste.

To serve: spoon over jasmine or basmati rice and top with chopped cilantro. Accompany with Thai roti flatbread.

Serves 6.

*Kaffir lime leaves may be found in Asian markets. If lime leaves are unavailable, substitute 1 tsp (5 mL) lime zest.

Pumpkin Gnocchi with Cambozola Cream Sauce

Tempest Restaurant, Wolfville, NS

"Gnocchi" is Italian for "little dumplings" and these tasty bites are traditionally made with flour and potatoes. For his autumn menu Michael Howell, chef and owner of Tempest Restaurant, adds pumpkin purée to his gnocchi and serves it with delicious Creamy Cambozola Sauce and Tomato Concasse.

1 ½ cups (375 mL) pumpkin purée
2/3 cup (150 mL) mashed potato
1 egg, beaten
1 ½ cups (375 mL) all-purpose flour
½ tsp (2 mL) salt
pinch each, ground nutmeg and Chinese five-
    spice powder
additional all-purpose flour for kneading and
    dusting
chopped chives, for garnish
Cambozola Cream Sauce (recipe follows)
Tomato Concasse (recipe follows)

In a bowl, whisk together pumpkin, potato, and egg.

In a large bowl, combine flour, salt, and spices; make a well in the centre. Add pumpkin to flour and, working with your hands, incorporate flour until mixture can be formed into a ball. On a lightly floured surface, knead the mixture for 3 to 4 minutes, adding more flour if necessary to keep from sticking.

Divide dough into 4 pieces, and using the palms of your hands, roll each piece into a coil about ½ in (1 cm) in diameter. Cut into 1-in (2.5-cm) lengths. Dust lightly with flour and press between your fingers to make a small indentation. Set aside on a lightly floured surface until ready to cook.

Bring a large pot of salted water to a boil. Working in batches, add the gnocchi to water; cook until the gnocchi rise to the top and are tender but still slightly firm. Remove with a slotted spoon, and cool. Repeat process until all are cooked.

Add cooked gnocchi to Cambozola Cream Sauce and return to serving temperature.
To serve: portion gnocchi on serving plates and top with Tomato Concasse and freshly chopped chives.

Makes 4 entrées or 6 to 8 first-course dishes.

Cambozola Cream Sauce:

1 cup (250 mL) white wine

1 tbsp (15 mL) minced shallot

1 cup (250 mL) heavy cream (35% m.f.)

1 cup (250 mL) pumpkin purée

6 oz (185 g) Cambozola cheese, rind removed,
  cubed

pinch ground nutmeg

½ tsp (2 mL) ground coriander

2 dashes Tabasco sauce

salt

Combine wine and shallot in a saucepan over
medium heat. Bring to a low boil and reduce by
half. Add cream and reduce by half. Add
remaining ingredients; stir until cheese melts
and sauce is smooth. Adjust seasoning with salt
if necessary. Makes 2 cups (500 mL).

Tomato Concasse:

2 medium ripe tomatoes

pinch granulated sugar

salt and pepper

Halve tomatoes, remove seeds, and finely dice.
Remove to a bowl and season with sugar, salt,
and pepper.

Makes 1 ½ cups (375 mL).

Grilled Shrimp and
Scallops on Pumpkin Purée

The Old Orchard Inn, Greenwich, NS

The dining room at the Old Orchard Inn overlooks the lush farms of the area, and the menu reflects the availability of seasonal produce. In this dish chef Joe Gillis skillfully marries pumpkin and shellfish — it is not only innovative, but also beautiful in its presentation.

⅔ cup (150 mL) pumpkin purée
¼ cup (60 mL) pure maple syrup
salt and pepper
12 raw shrimp, shelled and deveined
12 sea scallops
2 tbsp (30 mL) vegetable oil
1 cup (250 mL) Thai sweet red chili sauce
1 lemon, cut in wedges as garnish
Vegetable Flames (recipe follows)

In a bowl, combine pumpkin purée and maple syrup; heat in a microwave. Season to taste with salt and pepper, and reserve.

Rinse shrimp and scallops, and pat dry. In a skillet, heat oil over medium-high and sauté seafood until barely cooked, about 3 minutes. In a separate non-stick frying pan, heat chili sauce to serving temperature and add seafood.

To serve: spoon 2 tablespoons (30 mL) pumpkin purée onto each plate. Top with shrimp and scallops. Drizzle chili sauce around plates, and garnish with a lemon wedge and vegetable flames.

Serves 4.

Vegetable Flames:
2 cups (500 mL) vegetable oil for deep frying
1 parsnip, peeled
1 sweet potato, peeled
salt and pepper

Heat oil to 375°F (190°C) in a deep fryer.

Holding the vegetables firmly in one hand, cut lengthwise into strips with a vegetable peeler, using firm pressure. Deep-fry vegetable strips in deep fryer until crisp, about 1 to 2 minutes. Drain on paper towels and season with salt and pepper.

Red Kuri Squash Ravioli
with Seared Trout and
Braised Radicchio

Raincity Grill, Vancouver, BC

Andrea Carlson, chef de cuisine at Raincity Grill, likes to use red Kuri squash for this innovative entrée. This squash, originally from Japan, is noted for its smooth dry flesh and delicate chestnut flavour.

1 ½ lb (750 g) red Kuri squash (or other winter squash of choice)
salt and pepper
Ravioli Dough (recipe follows) or 12-oz (375-g) package thin fresh pasta sheets
2 tbsp (30 mL) hazelnut oil, divided
6 pieces trout fillet, 4 oz (125 g) each
¼ cup (60 mL) toasted, peeled, and chopped hazelnuts
2/3 cup (150 mL) chopped pancetta
3 shallots, thinly sliced
1 cup (250 mL) white wine, reduced to ¼ cup (60 mL)
3 cups (750 mL) torn radicchio leaves
salt and pepper (2nd amount)

Preheat oven to 350°F (180°C).

Cut squash in half and remove seeds and stringy fibres. Place halves, cut side down, on a rimmed baking sheet, pierce skin, and bake 1 ½ to 2 hours, until soft. Cool slightly; remove pulp and purée in a food processor. Adjust seasoning with salt and pepper. Remove to a cheesecloth bag and hang to drain overnight.

Prepare ravioli dough. Working in batches, roll dough to #5 on a pasta machine. Place dough sheet in ravioli press, fill with squash mixture and seal with another layer of dough. Cut into squares or circles and set aside, covered. Repeat process for remaining sheets.

If using packaged pasta sheets, cut into 3-in (8-cm) circles with a biscuit cutter. Place 1 tablespoon (15 mL) of squash in the center of each round, moisten the edges with water, and top with second piece of pasta. Press edges together firmly with the tines of a fork.

Heat 1 tablespoon (15 mL) of hazelnut oil in a skillet over medium-high heat; add trout and sear until just cooked, about 2 minutes per side. Remove trout from skillet and keep warm. Add pancetta to skillet and sauté until crisp; add shallots and cook 2 minutes. Add reduced white wine, radicchio, and hazelnuts and stir to combine. Adjust seasoning with salt and pepper.

Cook ravioli in a large saucepan of salted water for 3 to 5 minutes, until tender.

To serve: mound greens in 6 individual serving bowls, portion ravioli on greens, and place trout fillet on top. Drizzle with remaining hazelnut oil.

Serves 6.

Ravioli Dough:
1 ¼ cups (300 mL) semolina flour
½ tsp (2 mL) salt
2 eggs
2 tbsp (30 mL) vegetable oil

In a food processor, combine flour and salt; pulse to combine. Add eggs and oil, and process until mixture leaves the side of the bowl and forms a soft ball. Wrap dough with plastic wrap and let rest for 30 minutes.

Squash Ravioli
in Sherry Cream

Deco Restaurant, Halifax, NS

Rich and creamy, this decadent recipe created by chef Peter Kennedy is an excellent vegetarian entrée. He notes that fresh pasta sheets work just as well as the wonton wrappers, and suggests you roast the garlic for the Sherry Cream Sauce while baking the squash.

2 lb (1 kg) butternut squash
½ cup (125 mL) sliced onion
½ tbsp (7 mL) finely chopped garlic
2 tbsp (30 mL) butter
pinch fresh thyme, chopped
pinch each ground cinnamon and nutmeg
½ tbsp (7 mL) liquid honey
¼ cup (60 mL) grated Parmesan cheese
salt and pepper
1 pkg round wonton wrappers
toasted walnut halves, for garnish
Stilton cheese, crumbled, for garnish
Sherry Cream Sauce (recipe follows)

Preheat oven to 350°F (180°C).

Halve squash and remove seeds; roast on a rimmed baking sheet, cut side down, until tender, about 45 minutes. Remove pulp and purée in a food processor until smooth. Remove to a large bowl.

While squash is baking, heat butter in a skillet and sauté onion and garlic until translucent. Cool, then process in food processor until finely chopped. Add to pumpkin and stir in herbs, honey, and Parmesan. Season the mixture with salt and pepper.

Place a wonton wrapper on a work surface and brush around the edge with water. Place 1 tbsp (15 mL) squash mixture in centre of wrapper; top with second wonton and seal edges by pressing together with the tines of a fork. Place wontons on a parchment-lined baking sheet and repeat process, making 18 in total.

Bring a large pot of salted water to a boil. Gently add ravioli, a few at a time, being careful not to overcrowd the pot. Cook just until tender and remove with a slotted spoon.

To serve: portion ravioli on plates, drizzle with Sherry Cream Sauce, and sprinkle with walnuts and cheese.

Serves 4.

Sherry Cream Sauce:

½ cup (125 mL) dry sherry

2 tbsp (30 mL) roasted garlic*

2 cups (500 mL) heavy cream (35% m.f.)

salt and pepper

pinch each fresh rosemary and thyme

Place sherry and roasted garlic in a saucepan over medium-low heat; simmer until liquid is reduced to syrup consistency. Add cream and reduce over medium heat until slightly thickened. Purée in a blender and, if necessary, strain through a fine sieve. Adjust seasoning with salt, pepper, and herbs; serve warm.

*To roast a garlic bulb: slice the top off the garlic, cutting through the cloves. Place, cut side up, in a baking dish and brush with olive oil. Roast at 350°F (180°C) for about 50 minutes.

Pumpkin Spatzli, p.71

Sides

Preparing these side dishes requires a little time but they are so worth the effort. For your next buffet dinner try the Breaded Pumpkin Slices with Tomato Sauce or Kellock's Spaghetti Squash, Potato and Mushroom Tart — your guests will beg for the recipes.

Breaded Pumpkin Slices
with Tomato Sauce

Lobster Shack Restaurant at Salmon River House Country Inn, Salmon River Bridge, NS

This is an easy vegetable side to accompany almost any main dish, especially grilled seafood and meats.

1 pie pumpkin, 2 to 2 ½ lb (1 to 1.25 kg), peeled, seeded, and sliced in 1-in (2.5cm) slices
2 eggs, beaten
1 ½ cups (375 mL) dry breadcrumbs
½ cup (125 mL) butter, melted
Tomato Sauce (recipe follows)
⅓ cup (75 mL) grated Parmesan cheese

Preheat oven to 350°F (180°C).

Dip pumpkin slices in beaten egg and coat with breadcrumbs. Heat butter in a skillet over medium heat and sauté pumpkin slices, in batches, until golden.

Arrange pumpkin in a baking dish, cover with Tomato Sauce and sprinkle with cheese. Bake until sauce is bubbly and pumpkin is tender, about 30 to 45 minutes.

Serves 6 to 8.

Tomato Sauce:
2 tbsp (30 mL) olive oil
1 medium onion, finely chopped
2 garlic cloves, minced
4 medium tomatoes, peeled, seeded, and chopped
1 tbsp (15 mL) tomato paste
1 tsp (5 mL) dried basil
1 tbsp (15 mL) chopped fresh parsley
1 tsp (5 mL) granulated sugar
salt and pepper

Heat oil in a saucepan over medium heat; add onion and garlic, and sauté until onion is soft but not browned. Add remaining ingredients and simmer, stirring frequently, 10 minutes.

Makes 2 cups (500 mL).

Pumpkin
Spatzli

Restaurant Le Caveau at Domaine de Grand Pré,
Grand Pré, NS

Whether you call them spatzli, spaetzle, or spatzen, these little egg dumplings are a delicious accompaniment to main-course meats. Executive chef Alex Jurt prepares the batter with very finely grated fresh pumpkin, but for the ease of the home chef we prepared the spatzli with puréed pumpkin. Chef Jurt also suggests turning the spatzli into a main course with the addition of seasoned sautéed mushrooms.

⅓ cup (75 mL) milk
3 eggs, beaten
1 cup (250 mL) pumpkin purée (or 1 1/2 cups
   (375 mL) finely grated fresh pumpkin)
1 1/2 cups (375 mL) all-purpose flour
2 tbsp (30 mL) butter
salt and pepper

In a bowl, whisk together milk, eggs, and pumpkin. Add flour in batches, stirring to make a stiff batter.

Bring a large pot of salted water to a boil. Fill the square container of a spatzli maker* with the dough and set over the pot of boiling water. Slide the container back and forth, forcing the small dumplings to drop into the water. When cooked, the dumplings will rise to the surface, about 2 minutes. With a slotted spoon, remove spatzli to a colander and rinse under cold water. Repeat until all batter is used.

Melt butter in a skillet over medium heat; add spatzli and sauté until heated through. Adjust seasoning with salt and pepper. Serve immediately.

Serves 6.

*If you do not own a spatzli maker, drop small bits of the batter from a spoon or pass the batter through the holes of a coarse colander into the boiling water.

Butternut Squash
Risotto

Sequoia Grill at the Teahouse, Vancouver, BC

This colourful side dish makes a delicious accompaniment to venison or pork. It works equally well as a light vegetarian main course when made with vegetable stock. As an entrée, serve with a salad and crusty French bread.

1 small butternut squash
4 tbsp (60 mL) unsalted butter, divided
1 cup (250 mL) Arborio rice
4 tbsp (60 mL) minced onion
1 tsp (5 mL) minced garlic
2 ½ to 3 cups (625 to 750 mL) heated chicken
   stock
¼ cup (60 mL) heavy cream (35% m.f.)
salt and pepper

Preheat oven to 325°F (160°C).

Halve squash and remove seeds. Place cut side down on a parchment-lined baking sheet; bake 40 minutes or until tender. Mash cooked squash and reserve 1 cup (250 mL) for risotto.

In a heavy-bottomed sauté pan, melt butter over low heat; cook onion and garlic, covered, for 5 minutes. Add rice and cook, stirring constantly, until grains are slightly transparent. Pour in heated stock ½ cup (125 mL) at a time and cook, stirring often, allowing rice to completely absorb liquid after each addition. Cook for about 25 minutes in total, or until rice is almost tender. Add the squash, cream, and remaining butter; stir to combine. Adjust the seasoning with salt and pepper.

Serves 6.

Spaghetti Squash, Potato
and Mushroom Tart

Kellock's Restaurant, Berwick, NS

Chef Kevin MacDonald of Kellock's suggests leaving the skin on the potatoes when grating. He serves a wedge of the tart as a side to accompany red meat or pork, but notes that when served with a salad, the tart makes an excellent vegetarian entrée choice.

1 medium spaghetti squash
1 ½ lb (750 g) Yukon gold potatoes
1 lb (500 g) button or crimini mushrooms, quartered
2 tbsp (30 mL) chopped garlic
salt and pepper, to taste
½ cup (125 mL) extra virgin olive oil, divided

Preheat oven to 375°F (190°C).

Slice squash in half through the circumference and place, cut side down, on a rimmed baking sheet. Bake squash until tender, about 45 minutes. Remove from oven and let rest until cool enough to handle; scoop out seeds. Using the tines of a fork, scrape out squash and place in a bowl. The squash will resemble strands of cooked spaghetti.

While the squash is baking, bring potatoes to a boil in salted water. Immediately turn off heat and allow potatoes to stand in water until cool. Remove potatoes and grate with a box grater into a large bowl.

In a skillet, sauté mushrooms and garlic in 1/4 cup (60 mL) olive oil until tender. Drain mushrooms in a sieve to remove excess oil.

In a bowl, gently combine potato and squash, and season with salt and pepper.

Heat remaining oil in a 9-in (23-cm) skillet. Cover the bottom of the pan with half of the squash mixture. Spread mushrooms over squash, leaving 1 in (2.5 cm) around the edge of the pan. Cover with remaining squash and press to form a tight seal. Cook over low heat until bottom turns a golden brown, about 10 minutes.

Invert tart into another ovenproof 9-in (23-cm) skillet that has been coated with cooking spray. Bake tart in a preheated 375°F (190°C) oven for 30 minutes. Remove from oven and let rest 10 minutes before cutting into wedges.

Serves 6 to 8.

Barley Risotto with
Autumn Squash and Swiss Chard

Hillebrand's Vineyard Café, Niagara-on-the-Lake, ON

The chef at Hillebrand's prepares this variation on a traditional risotto with pearl barley rather than Arborio rice. The nutty flavour of the barley is a fine complement to the squash and chard.

2 cups (500 mL) pearl barley
1 cup (250 mL) autumn squash of choice, cut in ½-in (1-cm) cubes
5 large sprigs rosemary
5 large sprigs thyme
2 bay leaves
1 tbsp (15 mL) white peppercorns
6 cups (1.5 L) chicken or vegetable stock
3 cloves garlic
2 tbsp (30 mL) olive oil
1 ½ cups (375 mL) chopped onion
½ cup (125 mL) chopped celery
½ cup (125 mL) chopped carrot
3 cloves garlic, minced (2nd amount)
1 cup (250 mL) Swiss chard, cut in 4-in (10-cm) strips
4 tbsp (40 mL) unsalted butter
½ cup (125 mL) Parmesan cheese
salt and pepper

Preheat oven to 375ºF (190ºC).

On a baking sheet, toast the barley in the oven until golden brown, about 8 minutes. Reserve barley. In a saucepan of boiling water, blanch squash cubes until barely tender; drain and reserve.

Gently 'bruise' the rosemary and thyme with the back of a knife and tie the sprigs together with butcher's twine. Tie bay leaves, peppercorns and garlic cloves in a cheesecloth bag. In a saucepan, bring stock and herbs to a boil; reduce heat to low and keep hot.

Heat olive oil in a large sauté pan over medium heat; add onion, celery, and carrot. Stirring frequently, sauté until slightly soft, about 4 minutes. Add minced garlic and sauté 2 minutes; add toasted barley and sauté an additional 2 minutes. Remove spice bag from hot stock. Add stock, 1 cup (250 mL) at a time, stirring frequently and waiting for the liquid to be mostly absorbed before adding more stock. Stop adding stock when the barley is tender but still slightly firm, about 40 minutes. The risotto should be very moist and creamy but not runny.

Remove from heat and stir in squash, chard, butter, and cheese. Adjust seasoning with salt and pepper.

Serves 6.

Butternut Squash
and Romano Gratin

Westover Inn, St. Marys, ON

At the Westover Inn chef Tony Gosselin prepares this simple gratin to complement either pork or beef entrées. He notes that peeled sweet potato works equally well.

2 lb (1 kg) butternut squash, peeled and thinly sliced
¾ cup (175 mL) freshly grated Romano cheese
salt and freshly ground pepper

Preheat oven to 400°F (200°C).

Peel squash and slice thinly by hand or by using a mandolin.

Butter a 9-in (23-cm) square baking dish. Place one-third of the sliced squash in the bottom of the dish in a single layer. Season with salt and pepper and sprinkle with one-third of the cheese. Repeat this process, alternating squash and seasonings. Cover with foil and bake 35 minutes. Remove foil and bake another 10 minutes.

To serve: cut in squares.

Serves 6.

Harvest Pumpkin Cheesecake, p.80

Desserts

Pumpkins are so much more than a seasonal decoration, and chefs across the country have proven their merit by incorporating them in these wonderful desserts.

Harvest Pumpkin
Cheesecake

Fireside Café, Canning, NS

Absolutely delicious! This cheesecake is so moist and light it is like eating a cloud of pumpkin mousse. Though this makes 12 to 16 servings, you must allow for seconds.

Crust:

3 tbsp (45 mL) granulated sugar
1 ½ cups (375 mL) graham cracker crumbs
⅓ cup (75 mL) melted butter

In a medium bowl, combine dry ingredients. Mix in melted butter, tossing to coat. Press crumbs over the bottom and up the sides of a 10-in (25-cm) springform pan. Reserve.

Cheesecake:

4 eggs, separated
1 lb (500 g) cream cheese
¾ cup (175 mL) granulated sugar
1 cup (250 mL) pumpkin purée
1 tsp (5 mL) vanilla
3 tbsp (45 mL) all-purpose flour
1 tsp (5 mL) ground cinnamon
½ tsp (2 mL) each ground ginger and nutmeg
¼ tsp (1 mL) salt
1 cup (250 mL) blend (10% m.f.)

Preheat oven to 350°F (180°C).

Beat egg whites until light and fluffy; reserve.

Beat cream cheese until smooth. Stir in sugar, egg yolks, pumpkin, and vanilla. Sift together flour, spices, and salt; add to pumpkin mixture alternately with the blend, mixing until combined. Gently fold in reserved egg whites.

Pour mixture into prepared crust. Place pan on a baking sheet and bake for 60 to 70 minutes, until cheesecake is just set in the centre and the edges are starting to crack. Remove to a rack and cool 5 minutes before adding topping. (Leave oven on.)

Topping:

1 cup (250 mL) sour cream
2 tbsp (30 mL) granulated sugar
½ tsp (2 mL) vanilla
freshly grated nutmeg

In a bowl, whisk together sour cream, sugar, and vanilla. Pour mixture over cheesecake, return to oven, and bake an additional 6 minutes. Remove from oven and sprinkle with freshly grated nutmeg.

Gently run a knife around the edge of the cheesecake to loosen from the side of the pan. Cool completely on a rack and then chill, loosely covered, 4 to 5 hours before serving.

Makes 12 to 16 servings.

Sticky Toffee
Pumpkin Pudding

Tempest Restaurant, Wolfville, NS

This easy-to-prepare dessert from the kitchen of chef Michael Howell is comfort food at its best! Elegantly presented at the restaurant with blueberry sauce, it is also delicious served with vanilla ice cream or whipped cream.

1 cup (250 mL) chopped pitted dates
1 cup (250 mL) boiling water
½ tsp (2 mL) baking soda
¼ cup (60 mL) granulated sugar
¼ cup (60 mL) packed brown sugar
⅓ cup (75 mL) butter, softened
1 egg
½ cup (125 mL) pumpkin purée
½ tsp (2 mL) vanilla
1 cup (250 mL) all-purpose flour
1 tsp (5 mL) baking powder
½ tsp (2 mL) ground ginger
Blueberry Sauce (recipe follows)

Soak dates in water with baking soda for 1 hour. In a blender, lightly pureé mixture; reserve.

Preheat oven to 350°F (180°C). Grease a 1 ½-qt (1.5-L) baking dish.

Using a mixer, cream sugars and butter until light and fluffy. Add egg and beat. Add pumpkin purée and vanilla, and mix to combine. Sift together flour, baking powder, and ginger; stir into batter. Add date mixture and stir to combine.

Pour into prepared baking dish and bake until toothpick inserted in centre comes out clean, about 60 minutes. Cool 15 minutes and serve warm.

To serve: portion pudding on dessert plates and drizzle with Blueberry Sauce.

Serves 6.

Blueberry Sauce:
1 cup (250 mL) fresh or frozen blueberries
½ cup (125 mL) granulated sugar
1 ½ tsp (7 mL) liquid honey
½ cup (125 mL) water
½ tsp (2 mL) lemon juice
pinch of salt

Combine all ingredients in a saucepan over medium heat. Bring to a boil, stirring constantly. Reduce heat to medium-low and simmer, stirring frequently, 5 minutes. Cool slightly.

Makes 1 cup (250 mL).

Pumpkin
Strudel

Le Caveau at Domaine de Grand Pré,
Grand Pré, NS

Great chefs adapt their personal recipes to highlight the best seasonal produce of the region. Pumpkin reigns during the autumn in Nova Scotia's Annapolis Valley, and chef Alex Jurt customizes his traditional Swiss strudel with an unusual filling of pumpkin and pear. We know his creation will delight your palate and leave you asking for seconds.

Pastry:

2 cups (500 mL) all-purpose flour, divided
¼ tsp (1 mL) salt
1 egg, beaten
½ cup (125 mL) milk
2 tsp (10 mL) vegetable oil

Sift 1 ½ cups (375 mL) flour and salt into a bowl; make a well. Combine egg, milk, and oil. Add liquid to well in flour and quickly work into a soft ball of dough.

Cover work table with a cotton sheet and sprinkle with ¼ cup (60 mL) flour. Pick up dough and throw it down on floured surface. Continue kneading in this fashion, adding remaining flour as necessary, until dough is smooth and no longer sticky. Place in a bowl, tuck with a damp tea towel, and let rest 1 hour.

Filling:

1 lb (500 g) baking pumpkin, peeled and seeded
4 pears, peeled and cored
6 tbsp (90 mL) butter
½ cup (125 mL) granulated sugar
⅓ cup (75 mL) raisins
⅓ cup (75 mL) heavy cream (35% m.f.)
⅓ cup fresh orange juice
2 eggs, beaten
¾ cup (175 mL) ground almonds
1 cup (250 mL) all-purpose flour

Finely grate pumpkin and pears. Heat butter in a skillet over medium heat; add pumpkin and pear and sauté, stirring frequently, until pumpkin is softened, about 5 minutes. Add sugar, raisins, cream, and orange juice; cook an additional 4 minutes. Remove to a bowl and cool to room temperature.

Stir eggs, almonds, and flour into pumpkin mixture. Add more flour, if needed, to obtain a stiff mixture. Reserve.

Assembly:

½ cup (125 mL) all-purpose flour
½ cup (125 mL) melted butter, divided

Preheat oven to 400°F (200°C). Grease a baking sheet.

Cover a work table with a sheet and sprinkle with flour. Roll out the dough with a rolling pin, using more flour as needed to ensure that it does not stick. Roll as far as you can until very thin.

Brush the dough with butter and spread the filling to within 1 in (2.5 cm) of edges. Pick up the edge of the sheet and let the strudel roll itself up. Tuck in the ends and transfer to the baking sheet, seam side down. If necessary, form into a crescent shape to fit on the baking sheet.

Brush with butter and bake for 20 minutes. Lower heat to 350°F (180°C), brush again with butter, and continue baking until golden, about 15 minutes.

Serve either warm or cold. If desired, garnish with vanilla ice cream or whipped cream.

Makes 10 to 12 servings.

Potiron Bread Pudding
with Hot Coady Syrup

Vineland Estates, Vineland, ON

Potiron is the French name for members of the winter squash family, which includes pumpkins. Aptly named, the skin of a potiron can indeed be as tough as an iron pot. We have used a hammer with a heavy-duty knife to break apart an especially hard squash, and confess to having even smashed one onto a concrete walkway. While these methods do work, we find it easier to prick the skin of a tough squash and briefly microwave the vegetable until the skin is pliable.

Made with sweet brioche bread, this pudding is rich and delicious.

1 large brioche (or challah or croissants), 1 to 2
   days old
6 eggs
2 cups (500 mL) heavy cream (35% m.f.)
1 cup (250 mL) granulated sugar
1 tsp (5 mL) ground cinnamon
½ tsp (2 mL) ground nutmeg
1 tsp (5 mL) orange zest
½ tsp (2 mL) salt
1 cup (250 mL) squash, finely diced
Hot Coady Syrup (recipe follows)

Remove crust from bread and cut in ½-in (1-cm) cubes. (You should have about 12 cups/3 L.)

In a bowl, whisk together eggs, sugar, cinnamon, nutmeg, zest, and salt. Add cream, and whisk to combine. Place bread cubes in a large bowl, pour egg mixture over top, and gently stir until all bread is coated. Cover with plastic wrap and refrigerate 30 minutes (or up to 12 hours).

Meanwhile, in a glass dish, combine squash and 2 tbsp (30 mL) water. Cover with vented plastic wrap and microwave until slightly softened, about 2 minutes. Drain and cool.

Preheat oven to 350ºF (180ºC). Butter a 9 x 13-in (23 x 33-cm) oblong baking dish.

Add squash to reserved bread mixture, stirring gently to combine. Pour into baking dish and bake 35 to 40 minutes, until just set but still quivering in the centre.

Serve warm or at room temperature, topped with Hot Coady Syrup.

Serves 8 to 10.

Hot Coady Syrup:

1 cup (250 mL) granulated sugar

⅓ cup + 1 tbsp (90 mL) water

2 tbsp (30 mL) molasses

¾ cup (175 mL) heavy cream (35% m.f.)

1 tsp (5 mL) vanilla

2 tbsp (30 mL) butter

Combine sugar and water in a 4-qt (4-L) heavy-bottomed saucepan. Watching constantly, bring to a boil, but do not stir. Let water evaporate and the sugar will slowly start to caramelize. As sugar is caramelizing, heat cream in a small saucepan. When sugar is light gold in colour, carefully remove from heat (the sugar will continue to darken). Carefully stir in molasses (mixture will bubble and spit); stir in hot cream. Let the bubbling subside, and stir until smooth. Add vanilla and butter. Serve hot over the bread pudding.

Makes 1 cup (250 mL).

Pumpkin
Crème Brûlée

The Blomidon Inn, Wolfville, NS

Rich, but oh so heavenly, chef Sean Laceby has created a winning dessert with this variation on a traditional crème brûlée.

1 ½ cups (375 mL) heavy cream (35% m.f.)
4 egg yolks
⅓ cup + 1 tbsp (90 mL) pumpkin purée
¼ tsp (1 mL) ground cinnamon
⅛ tsp (0.5 mL) ground cloves
⅛ tsp (0.5 mL) ground ginger
⅛ tsp (0.5 mL) ground nutmeg
¾ tsp (4 mL) vanilla
¼ cup (60 mL) brown sugar
brown sugar to garnish
whipped cream, optional

Preheat oven to 350°F (180°C).

Heat cream in a saucepan over medium heat until it simmers.

In a bowl, whisk together egg yolks, pumpkin, spices, and brown sugar. Gradually whisk in warmed cream. Stir in vanilla and skim off foam. Divide among four 6-oz (185-mL) ramekins or custard cups. Place in a large shallow pan and pour in enough boiling water to come halfway up the sides of the ramekins.

Bake until the edge is set but the center jiggles and a knife inserted in the centre comes out creamy, about 30 to 35 minutes. Remove from water and let cool on racks. Cover and refrigerate until chilled and set.

To serve: place ramekins on a rimmed baking sheet. Sprinkle brown sugar evenly over tops. Broil with a torch or under a broiler until sugar bubbles and darkens. Garnish, if desired, with whipped cream.

Serves 4.

Pumpkin
Ice Cream

Kellock's Restaurant, Berwick, NS

Traditional old-fashioned ice cream is made with an egg custard base to which various flavours may be added. The chef at Kellock's likes to serve this ice cream with mincemeat pie or mixed fruit and Kahlúa liqueur.

The heavy cream may be replaced with blend or whole milk for a lighter ice cream.

2 cups (500 mL) heavy cream (35% m.f.)
5 egg yolks
¾ cup (175 mL) granulated sugar
½ cup (125 mL) pumpkin purée
1 ½ tsp (7 mL) vanilla extract

In a heavy saucepan, scald the cream by heating to just below the boiling point. Remove from heat.

In an electric mixer, beat egg yolks and sugar until pale yellow. Add the pumpkin and vanilla, and mix to combine. With the mixer running, very slowly add the cream. Return the mixture to the saucepan and cook, stirring constantly, until it thickens slightly and coats the back of the spoon, about 5 minutes. Remove from heat and cool.*

Freeze in an ice cream machine following the manufacturer's instructions, or 'still-freeze.' To 'still-freeze,' place mixture in freezer for 45 minutes and then whisk for a few minutes. Return to freezer and repeat this step every 30 minutes until the ice cream hardens.

Serves 6.

*Cool in a covered container in the refrigerator overnight or, if making ice cream immediately, chill in an ice bath about 30 minutes.

Pumpkin
Pie

Evangeline Inn and Café, Grand Pré, NS

Fresh pumpkins abound in Nova Scotia's Annapolis Valley during autumn harvest. This small café's chef has developed a recipe that will rival any you have tried. In testing we used freshly cooked pumpkin but canned pure pumpkin purée works equally well.

2 eggs
⅔ cup (150 mL) brown sugar
1 ½ cups (375 mL) puréed cooked pumpkin
1 tsp (5 mL) ground cinnamon
½ tsp (2 mL) ground ginger
¼ tsp (1 mL) ground cloves
¼ tsp (1 mL) ground nutmeg
½ tsp (2 mL) salt
2 tbsp (30 mL) molasses
1 ¼ cups (310 mL) blend (10% m.f.)
1 unbaked 9-in (23-cm) pie shell

Preheat oven to 400°F (200°C).

Combine all ingredients using an electric mixer, and pour into prepared pie shell. Bake 15 minutes, then reduce temperature to 350°F (180°C) and continue to bake 35 minutes or until a knife inserted in the center comes out clean.

Serves 6 to 8.

Pecan Glazed
Pumpkin Pie with
Bourbon Cream

Inn on the Lake, Waverley, NS

This pie might just be the ultimate recipe of your dessert collection!

Pie Crust:
1 ½ cups (375 mL) all-purpose flour
¼ tsp (1 mL) salt
½ cup (125 mL) butter
3 to 4 tbsp (45 to 60 mL) cold water

In a bowl, combine flour and salt. Add the butter and work in with your fingertips until mixture resembles very coarse cornmeal. Sprinkle the water over the flour mixture 1 tbsp (15 mL) at a time, stirring constantly with a fork. Form into a ball, wrap in plastic wrap, and refrigerate for 1 hour.

Roll out dough on a lightly floured surface and carefully place in a deep 10-in (25-cm) pie dish. Trim and flute the edges. Chill for 15 minutes.

Pumpkin Filling:
2 cups (500 mL) pumpkin purée
½ cup (125 mL) packed brown sugar
2 large eggs, beaten until frothy
2 tbsp (30 mL) melted unsalted butter
2 tbsp (30 mL) heavy cream (35% m.f.)
2 tsp (10 mL) vanilla
½ tsp (2 mL) salt

½ tsp (2 mL) ground cinnamon
pinch of ground allspice
pinch of ground nutmeg

In a medium bowl, whisk together all ingredients until combined. Reserve.

Pecan Syrup:
½ cup (125 mL) granulated sugar
½ cup (125 mL) corn syrup
2 eggs, beaten until frothy
1 tbsp (15 mL) melted unsalted butter
1 tsp (5 mL) vanilla
pinch of salt
pinch of ground cinnamon
¾ cup (175 mL) pecan pieces

In a medium bowl, whisk together all ingredients until combined. Reserve.

Bourbon Cream:
4 tbsp (60 mL) unsalted butter
⅓ cup (75 mL) granulated sugar
1 egg
1 ½ tsp (7 mL) boiling water
¼ cup (60 mL) heavy cream (35% m.f.)
¼ cup (60 mL) bourbon whiskey

Melt butter in top of a double boiler set over gently simmering water.

In a small bowl, beat the sugar and egg until well blended. Whisk the egg mixture into the butter. Whisk in the boiling water and stir until the mixture coats the back of a spoon, about 7 minutes.

Remove from the double boiler and let cool to room temperature. Add the cream and whiskey and whisk to combine. Refrigerate. Bring to room temperature to serve.

Makes ¾ cup (175 mL).

Assembly:
Preheat oven to 425°F (220°C).

Lightly whisk the Pumpkin Filling and spoon into the prepared crust, leveling the top with a spatula. Whisk the Pecan Syrup and gently pour on top.

Bake for 15 minutes, turn oven down to 325°F (160°C) and continue baking until a toothpick inserted in the centre comes out clean, about 60 minutes. Remove from oven and cool completely.

To serve: slice in wedges and drizzle with Bourbon Cream.

Serves 8.

Index

Library and Archives Canada Cataloguing in Publication

Elliot, Elaine, 1939-
        Pumpkin and squash : recipes from Canada's best chefs / Elaine Elliot
and Virginia Lee.

(Flavours series)
Includes index.
ISBN-13: 978-0-88780-708-4
ISBN-10: 0-88780-708-9

        1. Cookery (Pumpkin) 2. Cookery (Squash) I. Lee, Virginia, 1947-
II. Title. III. Series.

TX803.P93E45 2006   641.6'562   C2006-904338-8

Photo Credits

Cover: Meghan Collins

All interior photographs by Ted Coldwell, except where noted below:
Trevor Allen: page 93; Gary Castle: pages 4, 6, 7, 8, 9, and 10; Norman Chan: page 13 (1st photo from top); Meghan Collins: pages 2, 3, 12 (1st and 2nd photos from top), 13 (4th photo from top), 23, 27, 33, 49, 59, 65, 77, 87; Michael Marschke: page 11; Rocky Reston: page 13 (2nd photo from top); Suzannah Skelton: page 12 (3rd photo from top).